ALEX
IS A LITTLE BOY

Phrank-Jack Masta Trayde

AuthorHouse™
1663 Liberty Drive
Bloomington, IN 47403
www.authorhouse.com
Phone: 1 (800) 839-8640

Published by AuthorHouse: 09/07/2018

ISBN: 978-1-5462-3905-5 (sc)
ISBN: 978-1-5462-3906-2 (e)

Print information available on the last page.

This book is printed on acid-free paper.

authorHOUSE®

This book is about the importance of kids with different needs here in the Bronx, New York. Kids that are being raised by single, working class mothers in the inner cities all over the world. Some of the proceeds of this book will go towards rescuing stray cats from the low income poverty areas located in the Bronx, N.Y. I will keep all receipts in a binder as proof of our donations.

This book is dedicated to Mr. Peter from Morris ave located in Da Boogie Down Bronx and to my fairy God mother Addah, wherever she may be found today. We met at a restaurant where I was working in the Riverdale area. Also, a great and special thank you to my mother and sister Victoria for supporting me and helping me raise my son. Thank you to everybody at P.S. 91 and the Green-Burgh Graham School for helping us grow.

Alex is a little boy that plays with many toys, but Alex does not like noise.

I remember when he was born, oh what a bundle of joy! He was so cute and he opened up his eyes and his mouth to wail and cry. I remember that, that little guy, yes my bundle of joy and my little boy made so much noise.

05/29/2011

Alex is my son and just like any ole child he likes to have fun but unlike his mother, out of the sun. After only a few minutes of play he would look for the shade and sit right under a tree. As strange as this could be he would always choose a dancing tree. The wind would blow and make the leaves dance oh so effortlessly. Almost like a ballerina so pretty with glee.

Alex's favorite toy is his train. It travels on a linoleum carpet
where it never ever rains. New York City, where Alex lives,
has many, many trains; many subways and trains!!

In New York City, there are some rainy days. Sometimes, it has even rained
in the subways and trains! Can you believe it? The rain should have gone
down the drains, but for some reason, it did not. And big puddles were
created in these poorly lit stations where people impatiently waited.

On a puddles-less, warm Summer like Winter day, Alex was taken away by his playful grandmother, known as the queen of spades. She whisked him away on this marvelous day to buy another toy for him to play.

This "queen" is his grandmother and she is also my mother. She has many names like Abuela, abuelita, guella y lita la viejita cual siempre lo lleva y lo trae de su escuelita.

My mother loves Alex very, very much. That's why she takes him in the subway to Toys Buy Us. We ride in that famous New York City "D" train. Remember? The trains where sometimes it rains.

I remember telling Alex that when the train comes, it makes a rumbling sound, and that sound made Alex jump up and down. When this picture was taken, Alex had decided to sit and pay close attention. With his eyes in a gaze and his ears at attention. He was listening to the sounds that were coming from the engine.

Now, on the **D** train express we began our short
journey to Toys Buy Us, so please listen carefully.

On that day, there were many people in the train and a tall dark man stood out, he was strange. He never sat down and he never turned around. The only thing he did was to dance round and around. He wouldn't stop dancing and everyone frowned at this tall dark unhandsomely clown.

And now grandma the queen without the crown took a look at
me and then looked down. Down at his feet, which never seemed
to be able to make full contact with the ground. Grandma's eyes
opened big and wide and her eyebrows shot up, as this seemingly
talented or untalented guy dropped his cup. But that cup was empty,
as empty as a cup can be. That's when everything became clear to
me. Oh yes indeed! That what was in his cup was not coffee.

Then we jumped off of the train scampering away from the man that was strange and headed to buy a toy. For Alex my little boy. He is not so little anymore he is huge like a tower his head almost hitting the top of the shower. He is 12 years old and very tall. Alex used to play with many balls. He would roll them on the floor because he could not catch and for his mother Al was not a good match.

I his mother, master of most sports played softball and handball in a big broken down schoolyard with poor basketball courts. Who survived on chocolate torts! I was the girl who wore high water pants they were so high that people thought they were shorts.

Oh what a fuss! We just arrived at Toys Buy Us, and Alex with his faces brings me to a total disgust. The happiest kid in the world that nothing was never enough. Because he thought that his life was so hard not knowing how tough was mine, it was oh so rough. He would ride in a comfortable car many times as I used to ride in a smelly city bus. Definitely not going to Toys Buy Us.

Alex did not choose a train today. He chose a 1000 piece puzzle, I thought it was a bit much. I looked at the box that he would not let me touch. Then we walked to the checkout line where Alex would huff and puff as he saw a lot of people holding a lot of stuff. Finally, we made it to the register where I paid and Alex had nothing to say. He grabbed the bag with little fuss then told us come on lets hurry and get out of Toys Buy Us.

Exiting the store we decided to go back home. Alex all happy and tired in the D train express that was filled with all types of people that were looking kinda stressed. On a train that runs on iron wheels and not rubber tires, as it screeches and it squeals filled with people that are real. It takes us back home back to the Bronx where Grandma is queen of her castle that she kept with so much hassle.

That's where both Alex and I reside. Him an only child while I am the youngest out of four. The skinny little girl with curls who lives behind the red door. The door which nobody likes to knock on any more. Not even for a cup of sugar which we hardly ever had or even for a cup of flour, as people walk by every minute of every hour. And Alex with a good face finally enters this place with bags in hands and a little grace. He sits and forgets about his new toy. He ends up playing with his cat that is not a toy but actually is his true and only joy.

Alex makes a face at every single thing, and that face makes me want to take a swing. I would never swing at my prince who has always been very hard at handling. I always carry him under my wing. But that is not the only face that he makes. He makes happy faces too one for me and one for you. And Alex my prince will end this story happy, smiling, giggling and laughing.

Printed in the United States
by Baker & Taylor Publisher Services